T0198978

A
GLORIOUS
MESS

WestBow Press books may be ordered through booksellers or by contacting:

WestBow Press
A Division of Thomas Nelson & Zondervan
1663 Liberty Drive
Bloomington, IN 47403
www.westbowpress.com
1 (866) 928-1240

Because of the dynamic nature of the Internet, any web addresses or links contained in this book may have changed since publication and may no longer be valid. The views expressed in this work are solely those of the author and do not necessarily reflect the views of the publisher, and the publisher hereby disclaims any responsibility for them.

Any people depicted in stock imagery provided by Getty Images are models, and such images are being used for illustrative purposes only.
Certain stock imagery © Getty Images.

The Holy Bible, English Standard Version. ESV® Text Edition: 2016. Copyright © 2001 by Crossway Bibles, a publishing ministry of Good News Publishers.

ISBN: 978-1-9736-7413-9 (sc)
ISBN: 978-1-9736-7414-6 (e)

Library of Congress Control Number: 2019913481

Print information available on the last page.

WestBow Press rev. date: 9/18/2019

WESTBOW
P R E S S®
A DIVISION OF THOMAS NELSON
& ZONDERVAN

A GLORIOUS MESS

Kim Joseph

There was a man
named Jesus
He loved to build
things with wood.

His table and chairs,
Looked beautiful there.

And his cabinets all looked very good.

His tools were
treasures, well used.
A gift from His Father above.

The file left a splinter
From the gap in the center,
But Jesus still used it in love.

His Chisel was chipped
on the corner,
It left a dent in the trim.

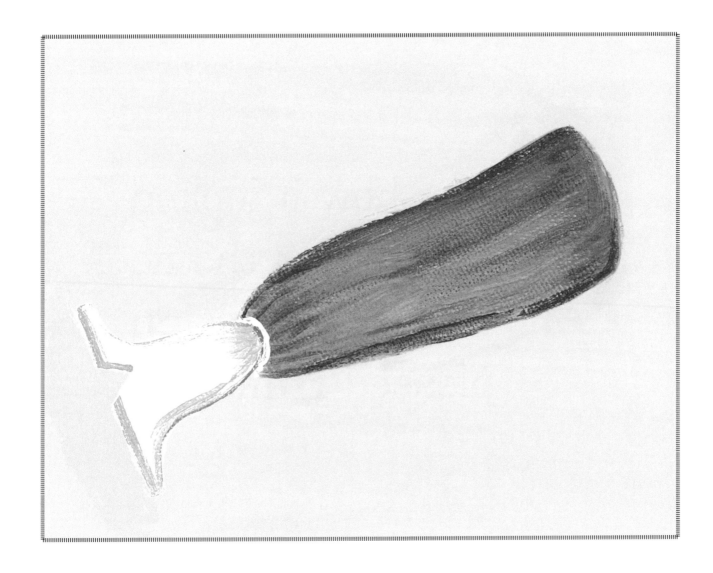

He liked how it looked
With the curve in the nook
And it's special design
pleased Him.

The saw he had used
many times,
Was missing a few little teeth.

And so He worked harder

to make a sharp corner

To make his Mom a wreath.

The girl was a cherub
with dimples
Her hair a tangle of curls
She knew she was loved
by the good Lord above
in her pretty pink
plastic pearls.

The little boy, ever so cute
with a few teeth gone
from his smile.
His freckles were glowing
his big ears were showing
and his heart was
as big as a mile.

we're all just a glorious mess
The Lord loves us,
just as we are
With quirks and bad habits
he still wants to have us
close to him, and not far.

So if you sometimes
feel broken
Remember this little rhyme.
For Jesus will still use you
And loves you SO much too!
No matter what,
through out time!

If we confess our sins, he is faithful and just to forgive us our sins and to cleanse us from all unrighteousness.

1 John 1:9 ESV

To my friend who loves me at all times.

Mary Routhe

*Kim, through thick and thin you've always been
the kind of friend that I wish was kin.*

Lynne

*I've known Kim for a long time. We've shared hard times
together, good things together, Years of praying for each
other and lots of Bible Studies. She's a great friend!*

Theresa Pendley

Kim has a heart of gold and compassion for others. This book is her beautiful way of sharing Jesus's love.

Rebecca Steapp

Follow-through: Kim has a divine gift to finish what she starts. It is most exemplary in her care for people. Love her!

Rachel Lugo

Kim is a lovely lady that is caring and considerate of others. She loves children, and has 2 lovely grandchildren she loves dearly. She loves church, and no matter where they go, you will find her looking for a church. She has a God given talent with what she does and I think this book will prove that!

Shirley Killion

Kim is the sweetest person I know!

Terry Waites

*Kim is a real talented person, who loves
life and reaching out to others.*

Sandy Cochran

*Kim is not only a wonderful and kind loving lady but
she is a true artist, she not only writes but she paints
also. What ever she does she does it well. I might also
tell you that she love's the Lord with all of her heart.*

Linda Hehmann

Kim is truly an inspired woman. She has been through life's struggles but never lets that keep her down. She has so much wisdom to give; I'm certain this is the first of many books.

Cassy Hupp

This book is filled with love for Joe,
Isaac, Cassy, RJ and Leah. <3

Kim is an awesome woman of God. "Application" is a perfect word to describe her as she truly applies Jesus to everything in her life. All her ups and downs are life lessons and blessings. She is always cheerful and deeply soulful. ☺

Patricia Bulka

Surviving a childhood of tragedy and betrayal that no child should ever experience can challenge the most steadfast among us. This book demonstrates Kim's faith in a loving God by offering hope to others using the innocence of a trusting child as the centerpiece of her work.

Susan Prenatt

Printed in the United States
By Bookmasters